Self Help Guide to Credit Repair

Stephen Steinberger

Self-Help Guide to Credit Repair

Stephen Steinberger

NOTICE

THIS PRODUCT IS NOT INTENDED TO PROVIDE LEGAL ADVICE TO THE READER. IT CONTAINS GENERAL INFORMATION TO SHOW THE READER THE STEPS THAT MUST BE TAKEN TO BUILD OR REPAIR THE CREDIT HISTORY. PLEASE CONSULT AN ATTORNEY TO MEET YOUR PARTICULAR NEEDS.

Copyright 2013 Stephen Steinberger and Eagle Publications.

Eagle Publications
Baltimore, Maryland

All Rights Reserved

Distributed by Eagle Publications

10 9 8 7 6 5 4 3 2 1

This book is sold with the understanding that neither the author nor the publisher is engaged in rendering legal advice. If legal advice is required, the services of an attorney should always be sought. Publisher and author cannot guarantee in any way that the forms and information provided are being used for the purposes intended and, therefore, assume no responsibility for their proper and correct use.

ISBN-10: 0615861415
ISBN-13: 978-0615861418

Important Facts

This self-help product is intended to be used by the purchaser for his or her own benefit. You may not reproduce in whole, in part, resell, or use it for commercial purposes without express written consent from the publisher. In addition to the copyright violations you will incur, the unauthorized reproduction and use of this guide to benefit another party may be considered the unauthorized practice of law.

This product is designed to provide authoritative and accurate information in regard to do-it-yourself credit repair. However, the accuracy of the information is not guaranteed, as laws and regulations may change or be subject to differing interpretations. As it happens, you may be subject to differing procedures from those contained herein, depending on where you reside. We strongly advise that you check local laws in your home state before acting upon any of the material in this guide, or using any of the forms or letters provided.

As is always the case where legal matters are concerned, common sense should always prevail when it comes to matters of a legal nature. We urge you to consult with an attorney or other professional that is relevant to your situation where large sums of money might be involved.

You use this product with the understanding that you act as your own attorney where necessary and that the publisher, author, distributor nor the retailer are engaged in rendering legal aid to you and shall have neither liability nor responsibility to any party for any loss or damage caused or alleged to be cause by your use of this publication.

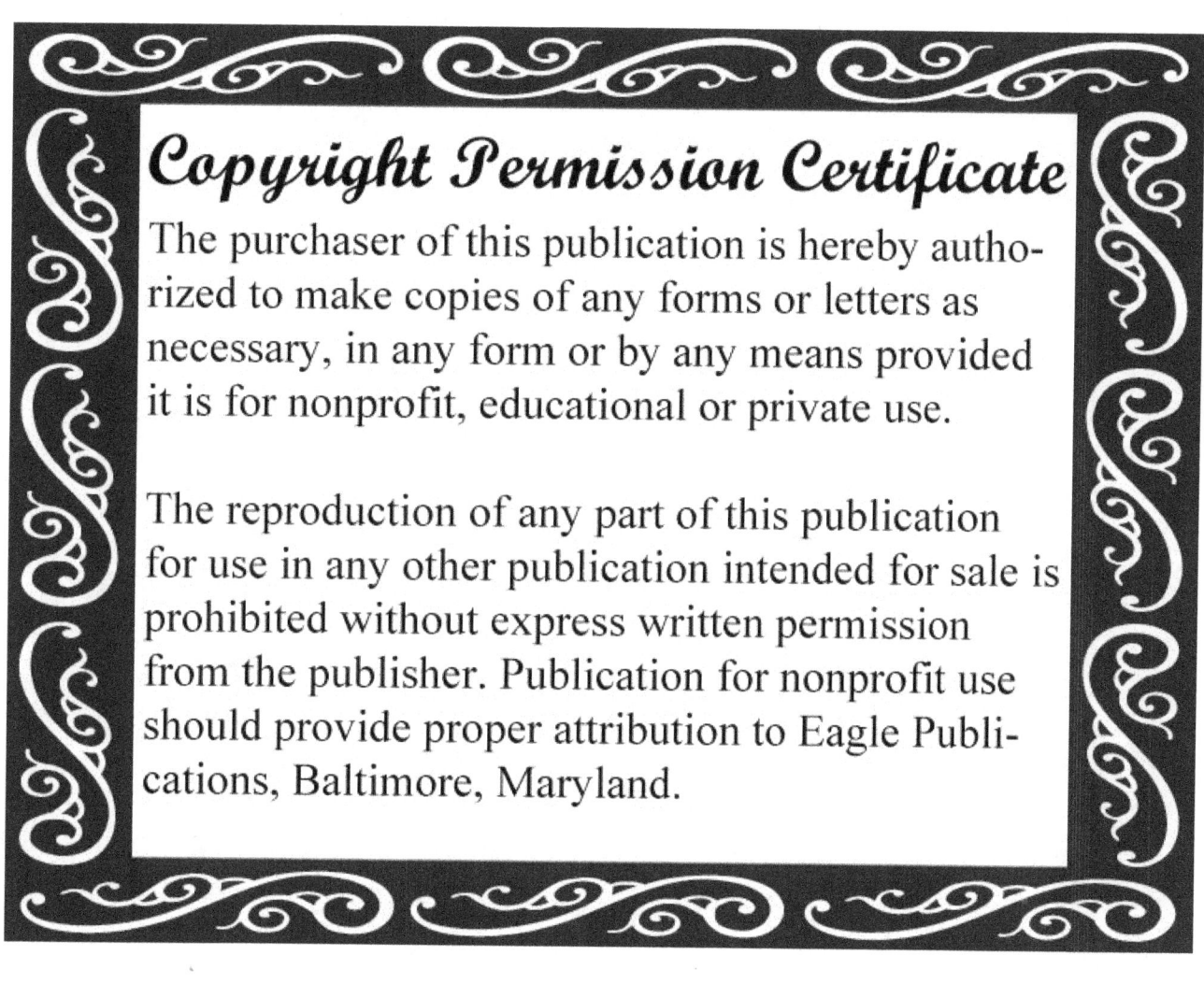

Table of Contents

Introduction
Test Your Creditworthiness
How to Develop AAA Credit
Obtaining Credit
Master Credit Data Form
Obtaining Credit
What Your Credit Report Discloses
The 10-Step Strategy to Repairing Your Credit
Gain Creditor Cooperation
Showing Charged-off Accounts as Paid
Letters in this Guide
Federal Credit Laws
Banks That will Open an Account When you are in ChexSystems
About the Author

Introduction

There is very little that you can do in society today without good credit. Many of the things that we want to buy, such as a car or a house must be financed, or bought on credit. Credit is even more important now than it was in the early 2000's, before the housing market bubble burst.

The problem is that it is very easy to ruin your credit, and once that is done, it can take many times longer to rebuild it than it did to tear it down.

Unfortunately, for the vast majority that has bad credit in today's society, it came about through no fault of their own. Bad things can and do happen to good every day. When the bubble burst on the swelling housing market, it was on the heels of a bad recession and the walls tumbled down.

People began losing their jobs; jobs that they had held for many years. Along with the loss of jobs, there was the loss of their homes. Mortgage foreclosures became so many, that lenders began a process of robo-signing paperwork, without checking to see that the paper work was valid, and the result was people losing their homes in some cases, that should never have come into foreclosure to begin with.

In the aftermath, the people found themselves not only with very little in the way of help from the federal government, but they also learned very quickly that they had to clean up the fallout from the whole debacle themselves. That is where this helpful guide comes into play. When you find yourself living from paycheck-to-paycheck, how are you supposed consider paying someone to help you clean up the mess. That's where the Self-Help Guide to Credit Repair comes into play for you. We show you how to clean up the entire mess. It will not be easy, and it will not be fast, but when you are through, you will find your credit report where it once was!

Test your Creditworthiness

Credit ratings are a way for a business to make a decision as to whether they or not they are going to grant you credit. The better your credit rating is, indicates to the creditor your wiliness to repay a debt.

The current financial world uses more than just credit reports to gauge you ability and willingness to repay a debt. Now a numbering system gives a more accurate picture of your credit worthiness.

The credit score, which ranges from 300 to 800, is based on a number of factors, including the information that is contained within the credit report. In most cases, a lender will not even consider granting credit for anything to you without a score of at least 600,
though there are a few who will go below that threshold, but those are the ones that will do so only if you pay a high rate of interest to them.

Credit bureaus ARE NOT allowed to give an evaluation of your ability to meet the requirements of repaying a loan or some other dent to the creditor. They are allowed simply to provide information that is contained in your credit history and the creditor must then make a decision as to whether they will grant you credit. While creditors likely do actually give an opinion of your credit worthiness, they do not do this publicly.

1. Evaluation of your potential: The criteria in your report are designed to give the creditor an accurate idea of where you stand as a credit risk. Borrowers will however, typically try to obtain items that are far beyond their typical financial reach. The institution entrusts loan officers to make decisions based on their experience and your credit reports/scores as to whether the company will grant you the credit required to get eh property that you wish to purchase. The loan officer will consider all of the details and fine points of the deal and make his or her decision based on the information that is in front of them.

In some cases, an institution will have an automated system in place that takes the human factor out of the equation, and credit decisions are based on software programs. In most cases, the company will not deviate from the decision that is made by the software, because the financial algorithm is designed to make accurate decisions based on your history.

2. Credit Scoring System: The credit scoring system takes into consideration a number of factors and establishes a credit score for you that is remarkably accurate. The scoring system tells a lender or creditor whether you will repay (or not) and it will even give them an indication as to whether or not the payments will be made on time. You will see an example of the scoring system later on in this publication.

3. Short Term debt to income ratio: Lenders use what is called the 20% rule when they make a decision about granting you credit. They will calculate which percentage of your annual income that you short-term income represents. They do not consider debt that is long-term type debt, such as the mortgage on your house when they calculate this number. Anything over 20% of your total annual income is considered excess debt. This may affect the creditor's decision in a negative manner.

> When you have a good idea of how you will be evaluated, you will have an understanding of what it is you will need to do in order to begin improving your credit rating. You will readily notice just where the weak points are as well as the things that are positive, that you can emphasize. You will also get a good picture of the amount of credit that you will be able to manage easily, based on your income, net worth, credit report, credit score and many other factors.

IMPROVING YOUR CREDITWORTHINESS

There are a couple of steps that you are going to have to take before you can begin to improve your credit file. Follow these steps first, and you will be on your way to great credit:

STEP ONE

The first thing that you need to do before you ever apply for credit is to check your credit report. This way, you can make sure that there is nothing negative on the report. If you are new to the credit world, you should still check your report to make sure that you have not been a victim of identity theft. This is a common practice in today's world, and thieves are making off with millions of dollars using the information that they have stolen from millions of victims. In most cases, it is actually very easy to get credit if you are new to the credit world, but if you identity has been stolen you have other issues to deal with.

Unfortunately, as with most other negative aspects of life, negative marks on your credit report will usually show up more consistently than the positive marks. This is because creditors hire credit bureaus to help them to avoid making bad loans. Naturally, your creditors and the credit bureaus tend to seek out the negative information about you than they are to ask about the positive.

It is your job to make sure that lenders see only the positive things about you. This means that you must do what you can (we will show you how further in the book) do to remove all of the negative garbage from your report. In addition to removing the negative marks, you must do what you can to get some positive information on the report as well.

STEP TWO

Try to score yourself as a credit risk. Most lenders will use a scoring system that helps them to establish the level of credit they are willing to risk based on your ability, or perceived ability to repay the debt. The loan officer of any institution, or the board if that is how they make approvals for credit requests, will disqualify applicants who do not meet at least the minimum score in this system. Every bank, or lender has their own method of scoring a potential applicant, and they keep these systems secret. Only the loan officer knows what the company is looking for in an application. A committee decides ahead of time what the score are, and they give the loan officer a bit of latitude to work with, and in most cases, the final decision to grant or deny credit to an applicant if left in their hands, allowing them to decide whether an application is approved or denied.

Creditors will often use these standardized systems to help to make the decision process more objective. For example, a bank will know, based on years of experience, that an individual who is at a certain salary level on his or her job will be able to handle a combined credit line of certain amounts on their credit cards. They have also learned over the years that people who move often, and do not have a phone or a steady job, are poor candidates as a credit risk. The questions on the credit scoring system have questions that are specific to these criteria.

Of course, the loan officers personal judgment is also important to the decision making process. However, the banks and other creditors try not to rely on the banker's subjective evaluation of a borrower. This sounds like a double standard, because they do put their trust in the loan officer's judgment, however, they like to retain final decision power. That, again, is how the scoring system comes into play and helps them to keep from making bad decisions when granting credit to an individual.

Remember that each lender or creditor has its own specific system in place and will ask its own set of questions. However, those questions are all designed to reach the same conclusion in the end, and will determine whether credit is granted, or not.

When you learn what the lenders are looking for, you will be able to identify certain areas of your credit report that you will need to improve and you can pinpoint strengths that will help to adjust your total credit image.

The Scoring System

Use the following test to score yourself and you will get an idea of how the lender, or creditor, will evaluate your risk as a recipient of credit. Answer each question honestly and then add up the points at the end of the test. When you are through, compare your final score with the chart at the end and you will get an idea of how it is done.

POINTS   FACTORS
Years at Present Job
0   Less than one year
1   Less than two years
2   Two to Four Years
3   Four to Ten Years

4   Over Ten Years

Monthly Income Level
0   Less than $1,000
1   $1,000 to $1,500
2   $1,500 to $2,000
3   Over $2,000

Present obligations past due
0   Yes
1   No

Total monthly debt payments compared to income
0   50%
1   40% to 49%
2   30% to 39%
3   Under 30%

Prior Loans with lender
0   No
0   Yes, but not closed
1   Yes, but closed, or with two or fewer 11-day notices per year

Checking Account
0   .None
1   Yes, but with over five rejected items in the past year
2   Yes, with no rejected items over the past year

Length at present or previous address
0   Less than three years
1   three years or more

Age of newest automobile
0   over one year old
1   less than one year old

Savings account with lender
0   No
1   Yes

Own real estate
0   No
3   Yes

Telephone in own name
0   No
1   Yes

Good credit references
0   No
1   Yes

These questions will be asked, or something very close to them will appear on the scoring systems used by creditors. The Consumer Credit Policy Committee chooses the questions and assigns points based on the answers given. They also prepare a set of guidelines to be used by loan officers so that they can apply the questions to the credit granting process.

Remember that the scoring system will vary from one creditor to another and will largely depend on current economic conditions both regionally and nationally. They will also depend a great deal on the competition the creditor3 is facing in your area at the time. When times are good, and the cash is flowing freely, these criteria loosen up a great deal.

Now, let us look at your score based on the questions you had to answer. In this particular example, you had the opportunity to score as many as 22 points. Going by the guidelines he or she is given, the loan officer might read something like the following:

0-11 points:
Reject outright. Do not waste time on this application

11-13 points
Review the application carefully. There must be criteria that indicate why granting credit is justified.

13-15 points
Review the application carefully with the intention of granting approval. Is there a reason why credit should NOT be granted?

15-20 points
Grant credit unless there is an indicator as to why it should not be granted.

20-22 point
Automatically approve within reasonable limits, based on income criteria.

If the score that you came up with falls into the lowest category, the creditor is not going to approve your application. You should not give up hope however, because you might still be able to obtain a small loan with some collateral or even a co-signer. (Co-signers use their good credit to help boost your chances of being approved by the creditor.) A good example would be a student who was working, but the employment was not steady because of school. His or her parents could co-sign for the auto loan and the credit would be granted. A co-signer can actually help a person with weak credit to rebuild their credit file as long as payments are made regularly, and on time.

If you fall into the 50-90 percent categories, you can expect that the creditor will give your application a full and complete review. While someone in the lower range of this category might require a cosigner or collateral, those in the upper range might find that their request for credit will be granted. If you find yourself in the 90-100 category, you will usually be unsecured credit simply by signing the application form or closing document.

Consider the scoring system carefully and remember that each bank will obviously keep its scoring system secret. The only person that knows how many points you will need to pass through the approval process, but once you have an idea of how the systems works, you will greatly improve your chances of winning approvals.

In the next section of this publication, you will learn how to develop AAA credit by following the five simple tips presented to you.

How to Develop AAA Credit

There are many reasons why you might be denied credit. For one thing, there may not be enough history for a lender to base his or her decision on. On the other hand, your credit history might be full, but complicated. In that case, you need to learn how to present your credit history to creditors in a positive light. Follow the five important tips presented here and you will be well on your way to achieving your goals. There are many ways to improve your credit report and score so that you can be granted credit. These tips will get you started:

TIP 1: Keep the 20% Rule in Mind

Only apply for the credit that you know you can handle. Look at what you owe to others and add up all of the short-term debt that you have. Short-term debts include things like installment loans, credit cards and other debts like those. If you have telephone bills that are outstanding and large, include those as well as any notes that are due within a year or so. Do not include debt such as your mortgage because this is considered long-term debt. Now add up your total yearly income and divide that into your total short-term debt.

If you answer is .20 or greater, then you are "maxed out" where credit is concerned, as far as creditors are concerned. This is known as the 20% rule, and the lower the number you ends up with; the greater your chances are of being approved on any credit applications. The creditor will look at this number very hard, and try to make sure that if they do grant you credit, the amount they extend to you will not make your dent to income ratio exceed that 20%. That is the reason you will hear many lenders, or consultants telling their clients to get that short-term debt paid down. Keep the credit cards, but pay them down each month. When you do this, you still have the credit available to you, but it is not showing as a short-term debt on your application.

TIP 2: Accentuate the Positive

You have to emphasize why the credit should be granted. When you fill out credit applications, emphasize those features of your credit record that gives a good indication of your credit strength. It is important to capitalize on your strong points by making them the focus of your credit strategy.

One if the strongest points you can make is having a good income history. The other thing is having a good record of accomplishment with the credit bureaus, your bank, the telephone company, and other creditors. Creditors like to see evidence of earning power over a period as well as a record of making payments on time.
When you are completing applications for credit, notice that the requests for information are much the same from one application to the next. In order to organize yourself for filling out credit applications, use the Master Credit Data form that is included in this publication at the end of the chapter as a reference so that you are giving the same information on each application and not just making guesses. The form will also serve another purpose to you – when a creditor calls for additional information, and some of them do, you will have the information that you gave on hand.

The Master Credit Data form will also help you to put your best foot forward by selecting the most appropriate data that will answer your creditor's questions. While you must answer all questions truthfully and completely, there are different ways to answer the same question and still be honest in your reply. You choose the way that puts the most favorable light on you.

CAUTION:

Whatever else you do: NEVER BE DISHONEST WHEN YOU FILL OUT A CREDIT APPLICATION! If you knowingly misrepresent yourself on a credit application, you are committing fraud and that is a serious offense.

Being selective however, is not being dishonest. Creditors are very aware of how financial data can be arranged to appear better or worse and they expect you to put your best forward as long as you stay within reason. If you do not, they may believe that your financial situation is worse than it actually is. For example, if you fail to check your credit references before the bank does, and they find that one of your references gives you a poor showing, the lender is going to conclude that this is the best that you could come up with and that things are much worse than you indicated they are.

TIP 3: Get a secured credit card

If you cannot qualify for an ordinary credit card or one that is unsecured, then try getting a secured Visa or MasterCard. A secured credit card is the doorway to establishing a good credit history. With secured cards, your credit limit is the amount that you have deposited into a secured savings account. This amount must remain on deposit for a period specified by the bank. In the event you default on the credit card, the bank then retains the amount in the savings account.

The downside of these cards is that most of them will charge annual fees. On the other hand, the interest rate will be lower than most cards because it is backed by collateral. In most cases, you will not have to pay an application fee for a secured card though there are some banks that do charge these fees.

The best place to apply for a secured card is through one of the major banks. Your own local bank may offer them as well and you may want to try there first. You can also look at most credit unions for one of these cards. Secured credit cards are the same as any other card. No one will know it is a secured card, regardless of where you use it.

TIP 4: Get a department store credit card

Apply for credit cards with one or more of the national chain stores. You only need a couple of these cards to build your credit history quickly. Many of the department stores will grant you instant credit simply by having a Visa or MasterCard. In situations where your credit history is spotty or non-existent, the major stores will often grant credit where others will not. Once you obtain a card and made payments for a couple of months, (make minor purchases to keep the cards paid down) use them as credit references to gain an additional credit elsewhere.

The most important thing you can do once you start getting credit with businesses, is to make sure that you keep the payments current. This will build your AAA credit faster than anything can.

TIP 5: Open a checking account

This tip alone will not get you credit, but what it will do is to give you a credit reference. Creditors look highly upon an application where the bank account question is answered that you have a checking and savings account.

Choose a bank that you would like to work with and establish yourself with them. If you are on one of the checking account databases like ChexSystems, Telecheck or Early Warning Systems, then it might be difficult for you to get a checking account. It all depends on whether or not your bank subscribes to one of those services. Over 70,000 banks subscribe to one service or another, but that does not mean that they will always use the service.

For instance, if you go into your bank and the person registering your account knows you, chances are you will not be checked out in that manner. Even if they do check you out and you are denied a checking account, some banks will work with you anyway. You will find a list of those banks in the resources section of this publication.

In any case, once you have established a checking account, keep it "clean". That is to say, make sure that you balance the checkbook each month and above all else, do not overdraw the account! This can turn out to be a valuable credit reference for you in time!

Successfully Borrowing from a Bank

Borrowing money from a bank does not have to be a difficult process. Bankers need customers just as much as the customer needs the money that the bank has to lend. Do not let the bank's formality intimidate you.

Bankers like to be in control of the situation because they are responsible for handling money that does not belong to them. The reason they give the impression that borrowing is serious business, is because *it is* serious business. For the bank's part, lending money, and on yours, borrowing, involves a great deal of responsibility from both parties. Do not let the formality and responsibility get in your way however, or prevent you from seeking the assistance of a loan from the bank.

Bankers are people too! They are also business people. If they recognize you to be well groomed and giving the appearance as being a responsible person, they are far more likely to take you seriously and consider your application in a favorable manor. If you give the appearance of being a choice customer, they are far more likely to jump in to assist you. Keep in mind that the bank is in business to make money, and lending money to people like you is how they do that. As a responsible person, you will find that you are quite important to them.

As you grow in ability as a credit entrepreneur you will need to have a good relationship with a local banker so no is the time to start cultivating that relationship. Having a good banking relationship can help you do more than simply obtain a loan.

These people have a vast knowledge of the credit world. Their job is to give credit to people just like you who are creditworthy. When you ask him or her proper questions, you can effectively use them as a free consulting service. The banker will be more than happy to give you the advice and information that you need in order to win your business.

Things to Keep in Mind:

Your own bank may be the best choice.
If you have a good banking relationship with your local bank, start there. A local bank offers you the opportunity to develop a good credit history. If you have a good relationship with your own banker, you have a slight edge over the prospective borrower who has no personal connection with his bank. Bankers can bend rules if they feel confident about you, even if there is a questionable mark or two on your credit record, or your income is not quite high enough to justify the loan you want.

Choosing a local bank may be helpful.
Even if it is not your current bank, choose a local bank. You will be applying to nationwide banks for many of your loans or credit cards in time. Citibank and Bank of America might not be in your neighborhood, and you do not have to start your search through them. For now, a local bank is adequate to start the ball rolling. Furthermore, local banks are far more likely to be receptive and pay more attention to you and your application.

Investigate many banks.
Do not simply stop at the first place that you come to. Even though you may be focusing on a particular local bank, you should still contact many banks in your area. If you are developing ties with a dozen banks simultaneously, the odds are good that one bank will come through with the credit you need. Nationwide banks may be too distant to visit in person. You can, however, contact them by mail. Many also have toll-free telephone numbers to enable you to get in touch personally. If yours does not have an 800 number and you do any significant business with it, the loan officer will be happy to accept collect calls.

Establish a personal relationship with a loan officer.

Bankers notice positive personality traits and, quite often, favor you with the benefit of the doubt. To gain the banker's personal respect, you must establish a personal rapport with him. It is important to deal with the individual loan officer with whom you feel most comfortable.

Do not be intimidated.

Never think of yourself as going to a bank to ask a favor. You are a knowledgeable customer coming to a discuss advantageous terms.

The meetings that you have with bankers will also serve to educate you further in the ways of the banking world. Just as an expert chess player becomes a master through playing many different opponents repeatedly, the more contact you have with the banks and other lenders the more you will learn as you develop your credit relationships, you will locate more banks and lenders anxious to extend credit to you.

Master Credit Data

Name:_____ Have you ever filed bankruptcy?_____
Address:_____ When?_____
_____ Unsatisfied Judgments_____
Phone:_____ Are you a co-signer, endorser or guarantor for others
Previous Address:_____ _____
_____ Outstanding Lawsuits_____
How long there?_____ _____
Other names used:_____ **CREDIT HISTORY**
_____ Creditor_____
Date of birth:_____ Address_____
Social Security Number:_____ _____
License Number:_____ Name on account_____
Employer:_____ Date opened_____Status_____
Address_____ Balance due_____Payment_____
_____
Years at job_____ Creditor_____
Position_____ Address_____
Supervisor_____ _____
Previous Employer_____ Name on Account_____
Address_____ Date Opened_____Status_____
_____ Balance due_____Payment_____
Years at job_____
Position_____ Creditor_____
Supervisor_____ Address_____
# of Dependents_____ _____
Monthly Income_____ Name on account_____
Other Income_____ Date opened_____Status_____
_____ Balance due_____Payment_____
Nearest Relative not living with you_____
_____ Creditor_____
Address_____ Address_____
_____ _____
Phone_____Relationship_____ Name on account_____
Alimony & Child support payments received Date opened_____ Status_____
_____ Balance due_____Payment_____
Bank accounts at this bank_____
_____ Creditor_____
Other bank accounts_____ Address_____
_____ _____
Real estate owned_____ Name on account_____
_____ Date opened_____Status_____
Mortgage Holder_____ Balance due_____Payment_____
Address_____
_____ Phone_____

Obtaining Credit

Most people who are emerging from financial difficulties consider it top priority to obtain credit cards, such as Visa and MasterCard, through which they can pay for day-to-day purchases.

Although it is possible to get a credit card without a good credit history or a high income, few people know how to do it. Most go through the ordinary process and are turned down for a card. Therefore, they incorrectly conclude that a Visa or MasterCard is unavailable to them.

Sometimes people with good credit histories and high incomes are turned down when they apply for several cards, yet they hear of people who seem less creditworthy who carry many cards.

The credit card world can be simple when you understand the rules that it works by, and they are not difficult to learn. On the other hand, it can be challenging and perhaps even mysterious to those who are uninformed.

The Credit Card System

You certainly do not need many cards to be successful. You must realize however, it is how you use the credit cards that give you wealth, not quantity. Though there are advantages to having many credit cards, it is the proper use of the cards, rather than their total potential dollars of credit available, that is important. At the same time, to get a number of the more valuable credit cards, you must know how the credit card system operates.

By studying the way banks interrelate, you will understand how to deal with credit card companies. You will find that banks work together to keep track of their cardholders. Most banks want to know how many credit cards you have before considering you for one of their own cards. They will find this information in your credit history when you apply, so you will put your best foot forward by being honest when applying. In any case, not every lending institution will issue you one of their credit cards. This is because many banks share a computer connection that trades vital cardholder information.

When banks become aware that you have too many credit cards they will automatically reject your applications. In the 1990's, credit card companies were falling over themselves to issue their credit cards.
This was labeled as a form of predatory lending and the companies were ordered to stop the practice because people were loading up huge amounts of credit card debt. During that time however, people would often get as many as seven or eight credit card offers in a single day offering credit limits as high as $5,000 or more from the start!

The bank card system

To make this clear, let us examine what might hypothetically be called the Bank Card System. When you complete the application at your local bank, there is a great deal more going on behind the scenes than most people realize. Although the name of your local bank will be prominently displayed on the credit card, there is a big chance that the card was actually issued by another bank. Because banks are interconnected, they trade favors and reciprocate functions. Most often, however, banks hire each other to perform different services. As a result, they create economies and save themselves money in the process. Processing a credit card application requires a bank to perform many functions it normally cannot afford to do on its own, so it seeks outside assistance
by using other banks.

The bank card system is complicated. Cardholders rarely gain insight into how involved the card-issuing process can be. First, there is the process of accepting the new applications, asking for credit reports, and setting up the approved accounts. Then there is card printing and embossing, as well as ongoing paperwork encompassing year after year of statements, sales brochures, late payment notices, and countless other details that make a credit card program successful.

Most banks cannot afford to support all of the functions that are required to issue and follow-through on credit cards. Therefore, to avoid the complicated and costly process, smaller banks act as credit card agents for the larger banks.

In other words, smaller banks contract with larger banks for card-related services. Many service packages are available. The largest credit card processing centers therefore does all of the accounting credit checks, mailings, statements, collections, and administrative details for the small banks. The fee that the smaller banks pay is a percentage of the annual credit card volume.

Most banks enjoy the benefits that they receive from this arrangement. On the other hand, many more banks are beginning to purchase their own computer systems to cash in on the big profits that come from functioning as a large credit card processing center.

The primary advantage of the Bank Card System is that it allows the smaller banks to stay in the game. Because there is fierce interbank competition, most banks must offer their customers the convenience of credit cards. This is such an important part of bank promotion that many banks make their credit card package a major advertising tool to attract new customers from their competitors. The Bank Card System saves the small bank from having to invest in computers and more personnel to compete.

The larger banks also benefit from the Bank Card System, because their overhead is partially subsidized by collecting the annual service fees from the smaller institutions using their card-processing services. In fact, card-processing centers often realize handsome profits.

Some bank networks link different parts of the credit card process in a kind of a chain. For instance, one bank may offer the card while another does the credit checks and a third (or even fourth) does the card embossing and monthly statements. Some of these chains may be short while others are surprisingly long. Most major banks may have many lines of agent banks stretching out in chains under them. Some of these chains extend through as many as three, four or five successive banks.

Applying for more than one credit card

What happens if you simultaneously apply for credit cards to a dozen banks in your particular area? It is highly likely that although through different chains, many of the banks will be connected to the same major bank, who is actually the creditor despite the fact that you are making payments to your bank. In this case, there will be one of two possibilities:

> ***The major bank approves your credit.*** The big bank may have a relationship with the agent banks that prevents the applicant from being approved for more than one card from the major bank. In other words, if you fill out an application with a dozen different banks that have a relationship with the same major bank, the major bank will issue only a single card, or account. Therefore, in the end, all of your effort put into filling out 12 applications will result in a single approval. More than one account is rarely allowed. Of the 12 applications that you completed, the first application will be approved while the remaining 11 applications will be automatically canceled by the computer system. The credit card will show the name of the bank that accepted your application. The biggest problem in this situation is that you have now generated 11 useless and potentially harmful inquiries on your credit report. Generally speaking, the more credit inquiries that appear on your credit report and resulted in a declined application brings your credit score down, and it makes creditors scrutinize you application a little less favorably.

> ***The smaller agent banks approve your credit.*** In a large number of cases, the major bank will issue several cards to the same individual. This is because the smaller banks have arranged to accept responsibility for the applications they generate in the case of default. It just depends on the arrangement the agent bank has with the credit card issuer. In instances such as this, the agent banks generate more revenue because they are willing to assume the risk of the default accounts that occur.

In order to determine which member banks do or do not assume the responsibility of the default accounts, you have to dig a little deeper. It is worth the effort however if you need to have several cards to build your credit faster, or to have the cards in your possession for whatever reason. (There are many people who have successfully managed multiple credit cards to finance a business start-up, for instance). Thoroughly research your geographical part of the country to gain greater insight into which Bank Card Systems can best serve your needs.

Shopping for credit cards.

Most consumers are surprised to discover they have many choices when it comes to choosing a bank credit card. You should examine all of your options carefully before settling on which cards for which you wish to apply.

Do not for one-minute think that all cards are alike, or that you must live in the same state to get a certain bank's credit card. Also, do not let anyone mislead you into believing that you must have an account with a bank in order to get his or her credit card.

As you conduct your search, you will learn that there are great credit card bargains all over the nation – as well as deals that you should avoid. Compare bank policies before you choose your cards. The following three features are a part of all bank card terms and should be reviewed before selecting the cards for which you wish to submit an application:

Transaction fees: banks have discovered that 50% of all cardholders pay their entire balance at the end of each month. This naturally limits the dollar amount of service fees each customer will be required to pay. To remedy this problem and increase their revenue, some banks have designed transaction fees that they have incorporated as part of their terms. For example, there are banks that charge a fee for each use of their card. Cardholders feel they are getting a deal because the annual fee was only $10.00 per year. This is not such a good deal for people who use their cards on a regular basis and they may opt to pay a higher annual fee instead of a per transaction fee. Credit cards of course, have changed over the years and the cards using programs like this have done away with them for the most part. Still, you need to read the terms carefully for any card that you apply for to keep from being surprised at the end of the month.

Annual fees: Many card issuers charge an annual fee for the use of their card. American Express is one of these companies, though they have come out with several products that do not carry an annual fee in recent times. An annual fee is designed for the card issuer to boost income for the sagging credit card industry. The banks feel that in order for the credit card industry to survive, annual fees are necessary because there are so many people that pay off their balances before finance charges accrue. People that have stellar credit will rarely run into a situation where they will have to pay an annual fee, though it does seem that these fees are beginning to make a comeback. If your credit is weak, whether because it has some dings or you do not have enough credit history, chances are you are going to pay some sort of an annual fee as well as higher interest rates. The bottom line is to do your research before you apply.

Finance Charges: As mentioned in the previous paragraph, those with weak credit, for whatever reason, will likely pay a higher interest rate than those who have good credit. The annual percentage rate varies widely from one card to the next and can be anywhere from 6% to as much as 29.9%. Use your due diligence. If you cannot find a card with a reasonable APR, consider opening a secured card account, which typically has a lower APR because you are offering collateral in return for the account. As you build a strong credit history, the bank will slowly begin to release funds back to you from the secured account, and you will have a card with the lower APR.

The best advice that anyone can give you is to always read the fine print carefully before you sign any application.

ATM and debit cards

The credit card field has changed dramatically over the last 10 years. Now you see almost everyone with a card bearing the Visa or MasterCard logo. That does not necessarily mean that all of these people have credit cards. Now, when you open a checking account, it usually has a check card attached to it that you use just like a credit card, except that funds are deducted automatically from your checking account. If your account has no funds, the card will be declined (unless you have terms that say otherwise). At one time, the cards were indistinguishable from any other – now however, they are starting to show as a debit card. If your credit is bad, or you have bounced checks in the past, you may not be able to get one of these cards. You must be able to open a checking account in order to get one. If you are in ChexSystems, or on Telecheck, the resources section will show you where you can check on obtaining a checking account if you appear on one of these systems.

How to get your credit cards

Here are seven essential tips to help you obtain the credit cards that you want:

Compile a list of banks

In the past, it was always easier to get credit cards in the state in which you lived. Now, with the growth of the credit card industry, you can get a credit card from just about any bank in the US as long as you meet their credit criteria. In addition to the national credit card companies that deal extensively in credit cards, you can also check regular banks and credit unions.

Get a copy of your credit report

Before you begin to apply for any credit cards, obtain a copy of your credit report. You are entitled to a free report each year from one of the major credit bureaus. Take advantage of it. You should really know what is on all three reports however, because there are known cases where one reporting agency has differing information from the others. You are going to need these reports anyway when you set out to do your credit repair work (if necessary). You can order your credit reports online by going to each of the following websites:

https://www.transunion.com

https://www.equifax.com

https://www.experian.com

Go online and apply

In the past, you had to call the bank or issuer in question and request an application. Now all you have to do is go online and most of them will allow you to apply through their website. Be careful when filling out applications however, and make sure that you only apply at websites that you trust and are displaying the typically **https://** prefix before the website address. In the rare instance that you cannot apply for the card online, you can usually apply by phone. Simply call the number displayed on the company website.

Apply for secured cards

If you have negative items on your credit report, apply for secured cards. This will help you to build a good credit history while you are working on removing the negatives from your report. If one of your reports does not have any negative items against you in its report, then try to find out which credit card companies use them and apply with those. While all of these credit bureaus are large, the one that seems to pop up most often is Experian.

Get the number of inquiries on your report down

Write a letter to the credit bureaus insisting that the credit inquiries be removed from your history. Generally speaking, the more applications you fill out, the more inquiries will appear on your credit report. Creditors will look at these inquiries in a negative light in most cases, so do what you can to have them removed using the letter in the letters section of this guide.

Apply for cards with retailers

It is often easier to get a store's credit card than it is to get one of the national cards. These cards include department stores like JC Penney and Sears, gas stations like Texaco and Exxon, etc. These cards all report to the national credit bureaus and will work toward building your credit history. Even companies like Fingerhut are beginning to report to the bureaus now, so those accounts are beneficial as well.

Consult a loan officer at your local bank

Ask the loan officer what your chances would be of getting a credit card with your banking institution. He or she will be happy to tell you what needs to be removed from the credit report in order to qualify for their bank card.

The most important thing to remember, is that if you do not qualify for a standard credit card account, you can always open a secured card account, get the same benefits and perhaps even get a lower interest rate. These cards still work to help build your credit history, even if you only get one!

What Your Credit Report Discloses

Credit reports may vary slightly between agencies, but they all give basically the same information which includes:

Identification information

Your full name, last two addresses, social security number, birth date, and your place of employment. The length of your employment and your income is not something that is displayed on the credit report.

Detailed account information

In short, if you have credit with a company and they report to the bureaus each month, that information will appear in this section, including the number of times your were late with a payment, etc.

Public record information

This information includes any bankruptcies, liens against your property, judgments, etc.

Credit report requests

Anytime a company requests a copy of your credit report for the purpose of granting you credit, these inquiries appear in this section. It also includes inquiries for preapproval offers too, which have now finally been limited by the government. Imagine, someone getting information from your credit report without having your permission! Work to get these removed because they DO affect your credit history.

Consumer statement

When you embark on your journey of cleaning up your credit report, the credit bureau must verify anything that you dispute within 30 days, or it must be removed from the history.
You will learn more about that later on in this guide, but if there is something that cannot be removed for any reason, you are permitted to have a statement added to the report that explains the reason your history is such as it is.
That does not necessarily mean that potential creditors will grant you an account based on that statement, but at least you will have had the opportunity to explain your position.

The five most common reasons for credit denial

When a prospective creditor inquires about your credit standing, they examine your record with certain expectations. To evaluate your own report, you need to know those expectations. The five most common reasons for credit denial based on a credit report are as follows:

Delinquent credit obligations

Put simply, you have now or in the past, been past dues with your payments.

Credit application incomplete

You left out some important piece of information when completing the credit application.

Too many inquiries

As previously mentioned, creditors tend to look negatively on a credit report where there have been many inquiries, which they translate into requests for credit that were denied.

Errors in your file

Remember, a human input much of the information in your credit file, and humans make mistakes. That is why it is important that you stay on top of your credit report and dispute inaccurate information.

Insufficient credit file

This most often occurs when the credit report does not have enough information on which a creditor can base its decision. Try getting a store card or a secured credit card to build your history.

It is important that you stay on top of your credit report and credit score. In today's society, identity theft is on the rise, and the internet makes it extremely easy for identity thieves to get your information if you are not diligent in keeping it safe. Get your credit reports (all of them) at least once a year and make immediate inquiries if there is something there that you know nothing about.

You can find a sample letter for obtaining your credit report in the letters section of this guide. There are certain instances where you are entitled to a free credit report including:

Free Annual Report
When you apply for credit and are denied

Be sure to follow the letter sample carefully, because the bureau will deny your request if they do not have all of the necessary information. Also, keep in mind that you can order these reports online if you have the means to pay for them online (for those that must be paid for).

The 10-Step Strategy to Repairing Your Credit

Now on to the likely reason you purchased this guide. Now that you have all of your credit reports, you can begin the process to repair your credit file. It is not hard, but it is time consuming. This is largely because of the length of time you must wait in between letters. The process will be much smoother if you create a folder on your computer. You can create a folder for each bureau and save a copy of the letters that you sent in each folder. Whatever is easiest for you is best. There is really no set method for doing this but it would look like this:

A main folder named Credit Repair
Inside of that folder, create three folders named Trans Union, Experian and Equifax.
Type master copies of each of the letters and save them in the main folder.
As you write each letter, simply customize it for the bureau in question, and then include the information that you are disputing, and then save the letter to its respective folder. Once you have all of the letters ready, print them out on your printer and then mail them.

The Fair Credit Reporting Act (FCRA) 15 USC sections 1681a through 1681t, protects you against credit abuse that might result in an unfair description of your creditworthiness. Knowing the following six basic rights is essential if you are to successfully erase the negative marks in your credit report and regain a good credit status:

Right #1: You are allowed to challenge the accuracy of your credit report at any time.

Right #2: The credit bureau must investigate anything that you challenge.

Right #3: The credit bureau must investigate the disputed information within 30-days. This became a matter of law on September 30, 1997. The time period begins when the credit bureau receives notice of the dispute from the consumer. The only exception to the 30-day period is when the consumer sends the bureau additional information within the 30-day period. The bureau may extend the deadline a maximum of 15 days in that case.

Right #4: If the credit bureau finds any error, it must promptly delete the erroneous information from its files.

Right #5: If the bureau cannot or does not confirm the information you have challenged within a reasonable time period, it must delete the information from your files.

Right #6: If the creditor verifies the information and the bureau responds in a timely manner, the negative marks must remain on your record. If you maintain that the information is incorrect, the bureau must permit you to write a statement explaining your position and place it on your credit record. The statement is usually limited to 100 words.

The 10-Step Plan

STEP ONE: Identify Your Credit Problems

The first thing that you need to do in repairing your credit file is to go through each report and note any negative remarks. Circle each one to make their easier to find when you begin writing your letters. The information in the reports will be coded, but when you order your credit file from each of the bureaus, they will include instructions on how to properly read the reports.

> A) The historical status is a record of the monthly payments that you make. Ideally, this should be free of any past-due symbols, which may be 30-, 60- or 90-day periods. Almost 90 percent of the bad marks can be from past-due symbols. These could have been entered accidentally, or because the mail was late, or because delays in processing your payments caused them to be entered. Of course, you may have made late payments; you must send your payments in so that the creditor has time to process them before the due date. This means do not wait until the due date to mail your payment in.

> B) The comments section of the entry may contain remarks such as charged to profit and loss statement or something similar. This means that the creditor has charged your account of as a bad debt loss and that it does not expect to collect from you. This, of course, implies that you are a bad credit risk.

C) Inquiries made by any bank, store or other company to which you applied for credit will be listed in the report. Too many of these may be taken by a potential creditor as an indication that you are in financial difficulty and may be seeking more credit as a solution to the problem. Creditors will refuse to give credit on the basis of too many inquiries. How many is too many, is subjective and will vary from one creditor to the next. You should never have more than two or three at any given time. Do what you must to have these removed. You will learn how later on.

D) Public records may appear in your credit report as tax liens, bankruptcies or court judgments. These records must also be thoroughly examined for their accuracy.

STEP TWO: Determine Your Overall Credit Score (do not confuse with your FICO score)

Somewhere on your credit report, you will find a column with a title such as Account Profile. This column contains a summary rating for each of your accounts. A summary may read positive, negative or NR, which means not rated. Even though an entry might be non-rated, it can still put a negative light on you. Each negative or NR entry will have a code near it describing the problem. Use the chart provided by the bureau to determine what the problem is with that account.

STEP THREE: Create a Protest Letter to the Credit Bureau Disputing Each Negative Item.

Next, you are going to write a letter to each credit bureau disputing the items that are negative on your report for that bureau. You must aggressively challenge each item on each report, even if you think it may be a correct entry. Under the Fair Credit Act, it is your right to dispute anything that appears on your credit file. In your letter, put why you think the entry is incorrect. The credit bureau MUST verify each entry that you dispute and one of two things might happen. First, if the creditor does not answer the bureau in a timely manner, then the bureau MUST remove the item
From the report, even though it might actually be correct. If the credit bureau does not act in a timely manner, the item STILL has to come off. The worst-case scenario is that the creditor verifies that the information is correct and it does not come off. You have a better chance of the item coming off the report than of it staying – especially if it is an old debt.

STEP FOUR: Send Your Letter of Dispute

Using the sample letters included in the letters section as your guide, draft a letter to each of the credit bureaus disputing the negative items in your credit report. The letter SHOULD NOT look like a form letter. List each item that you want to challenge. If you have any documents supporting your claims, include those too, but really, it is not necessary that you do so. When the letter is finished, make a copy for your records and then mail the original with a return receipt requested for proof that the credit bureau received it. Sample letter three should be used to dispute negative items. Sample letter four should be used to remove outdated information. Use sample letter five to remove excessive inquiries from your credit report.

STEP FIVE: Log Your Activity

Create a log and note the date that you sent the letters to each bureau. Note the information that you disputed or requested to be removed.

STEP SIX: Wait for Your Response

The credit bureau must respond to you within 30 days.

STEP SEVEN: Send Follow-up Letters

If the credit bureau does not respond within a reasonable amount of time, write and mail your follow-up letters. Be sure to log each letter you send in this stage just like the first. Use sample letter 6 as your guide for the first reminder. This is usually enough to light a fire under the butts of the credit bureau. Tell them that you want an updated credit report once the information has been addressed. If they do not respond to sample letter six, then move on to sample letter seven and send that out. If they still do not respond, send sample letter 8 out and demand that the information in question be removed from your credit report due to their failure to respond in a timely manner. In the event credit bureau still fails to respond (this is unusual), then let them know that you will be contacting the Subcommittee on Banking, Credit and Insurance as well as the Federal Trade Commission, who has the ability to bring action against the credit bureau (do not say that part). You may also point out to them that the credit bureau may be liable for damages resulting from further issuance of the old credit report, and that they may also be liable for attorney's fees when you retain your lawyer to handle the issue for you. As previously mentioned however, it is highly unusual for this to get that far.

STEP EIGHT: Ask for an Updated Report

As mentioned in step seven, in your letters to the bureau, tell them that you are entitled to an updated report when the information has been updated. 15 USC 1681j of the FCRA requires the bureau to send you an updated copy of the report to you when the information has been addressed. The bureau is only required to send you a copy of the updated information; however, it is usually more convenient for them to send you a new copy of the entire report.

STEP NINE: Compare the New Report with the Old Report

Most bureaus will automatically send you an updated report. When they do, compare the new report with the old one and then start the removal request process over again. There is a good chance that you will not get results on every disputed item the first time around, so you have to follow-up. Notice that the bureau has responded to some of your items without a response from the creditor. This is because the creditor failed to respond in a time manner, so you are using this fact to your advantage. Everything that you successfully have removed from your report is a plus in your favor. This is common because the creditor does not want to invest the time with the bothersome paperwork.

STEP TEN: Repeat the process

Send out all letters after you mark off the negatives on your new credit report. Again, make sure that you keep records of all disputes in your log, and stay on top of things. Within a year, you could potentially have enough information removed from your credit report to make it look highly favorable to creditors. This is extremely important, in case your first round of letters uncovers more information from a particular creditor that was more damaging than it was to begin with. Be persistent however. It WILL work in your favor!

Gain Creditor Cooperation

Many times, dings cannot be removed from the credit report simply because the information is accurate and the creditor updates it as such. Your goal then becomes working to persuade the creditor to soften their stance by either toning down or entirely deleting their remarks on your credit report. When the letter writing is complete, the nest step is to get creative and convince the creditor to remove damaging remarks and
information. Right now, we simply want to turn those current bad debts into positive information. You can do just that by following these eight steps:

STEP ONE: Setup a Worksheet for Each Creditor

Accurate record keeping is an essential part of your dealings with the creditors who still give you bad ratings. Use a creditor worksheet containing names, account numbers, credit remarks and any other documents, correspondence or notes you have on dealings with them.

STEP TWO: Write to Each Creditor

After studying all of the facts concerning each account and nature of the credit complaints, write each creditor explaining your version of how the problem arose to begin with. Use sample letter 9 as a guide but do not be afraid to expand on it a bit. Be specific and give all of the relevant details, including full documentation. Be factual, but you want to appeal to the creditor's sense of goodwill. Perhaps your company went bankrupt suddenly, or you lost your job. Maybe you were detained for several weeks in a foreign country while you were on a business trip and that rendered you unable to pay your bills on time. Remind the creditor that you eventually paid, and mention that you appreciated his or her services and products despite the fact that payment issues arose. Appeal to the creditor's compassion; ask that the bad marks be removed now that the account is settled, or ask the creditor to put a statement into your credit report acknowledging that the account is paid up. Most will actually have already done this, but many may not have taken the time to do so.

As you write the letter, consider it in light of your other accounts that may have been affected by the same circumstances. Each letter you send should be consistent with the others so that, if your creditors' new comments appear on the credit file, they will appear reasonable and consistent.
Do not send in weak excuses for late bill-paying habits. Use strong, compelling reasons. Send the letter by certified mail, return receipt requested. It is a little more expensive to mail it this way, but it will give an accurate record of your contact with the creditor. Enter the contact information into your log.

STEP THREE: Order an Updated Credit Report after 30 Days

Your letters just might do the trick and convince creditors to remove the negative dings from your credit report. Be sure to wait at least 30-days before requesting the new credit report. Have the bad marks been deleted? Did the creditor at the very least, soften the remarks and/or note that the account has been satisfied?

STEP FOUR: Contact the Creditor by Phone

If your letters seem futile, or go unanswered, use the telephone to achieve your goals. This will allow you to interact with the creditor on a more personal level. Before you make any calls, study the information that you gathered from your credit report, the responses from your creditor and the worksheet that you compiled. Next, write a simple outline of the points that you wish to discuss with the creditor. Sometimes, people can be rude. Keep in mind that as long as you remain professional and do not raise your voice, there is a good chance that you will be able to reach your goals. Getting angry, raising your voice and cursing at your creditor on the phone will do nothing to help your cause!

STEP FIVE: Be Persistent

In many cases, your first call to the creditor will fall on deaf ears and have no result. The key is to be persistent and do not get discouraged. Try again. If you are dealing with a large company, chances are you will not get the same person twice. This increases your chances of getting a negative removed from the credit report. Once you get a creditor to agree that the change in your credit report is justified, ask on the phone that the change be made in your credit status. Offer to send the creditor a letter with that agreement in writing, along with a self-addressed, stamped envelope. Be sure to get the creditors name and office mailing address, preferably, you will get the opportunity to send the letter directly to the person you have spoken with. The creditor can then sign the letter and date it. They can then return it to you for your records and you will be able to use this when contacting creditors for new accounts. You will also be able to send the letter to the credit bureau if the creditor forgets to remove the ding from your report.

STEP SIX: Send Your Statement to the Credit Bureau

After some time passes and the creditor still has not softened the report or removed the ding from your credit file, write a letter to the credit bureau and ask that they include a consumer statement on your credit file. 15 USC 1681i of the FCRA requires that they allow you to do this. Your comments as to why the bill was not paid on time will then be submitted with your credit report in response to any credit request.
Your comments may greatly mitigate the damage of that particular entry. When you submit your statement, refrain from commenting on just one particular ding. Instead, make the statement one in general that explains generally the reason for the poor report. For example, if you have several negative entries on your credit report, are they because:

    A layoff from your job?
    Divorce?

Personal or Family Illness?
Tax Problems?
Some other reason?

These unfortunate experiences can hit anyone, and in the financial recession that hit almost worldwide back in 2007/2008 it pretty near did. People who were tenured in their jobs and were virtually guaranteed a stable position were losing their jobs left and right. Unemployment was so bad that the federal government extended unemployment benefits three times for millions of US residents.

STEP SEVEN: Wait the Estimate Time for a Response

The ball is now back in the credit bureau's court. Be sure to give them ample opportunity to respond. In a few weeks' time, the bureau should respond to you about your query and they may even include an updated copy of your credit report as well.

STEP EIGHT: Try Again

Remember: persistence is the key to successfully removing the negative items from your credit report. Whether it is having negative dings removed, or having creditors to remove the dings for you, your persistence will be rewarded with results. After several months have passed, try having any remaining negatives removed again. It could be that personnel changes have been made in the office of the creditor for those who still would not remove any negatives and the person that you find there now might be more receptive to your query. Keep at it until you have everything remove from your report. It CAN and DOES happen every day. The results that you end up with are going to be much better than paying lawyers or credit repair companies who will stop at a single round of letters and queries to your creditors. The results you end up with after the initial and follow-up letters are all the credit repair companies will do, and if you want them to do the process again, you have to pay them again!

Showing Charged-Off Accounts as Paid

By now, your credit report is showing marked improvement. The next thing that you have to do however is to remove bad debts from the report, if there is anything there. Regardless of the fact that an account has been turned over for collections, you can still turn the negative into a positive.

Debt collectors are working for one of two fees: Some are actively collecting for the original creditor, and will receive part of the collected amount, which ranges anywhere, from 35 percent to as much as 50 percent. Other collectors buy the charged off accounts from the creditor for pennies on the dollar. In any case, you can usually make a deal with them and pay only a portion of the actual debt, and have it reported as paid in full to the creditor in question.

The first thing that you need to do is to contact the party in question. Negotiate with them, starting with a low number and forcing them to make a counter offer. For instance, if the debt is in collections, offer to pay 25 percent of the amount in a single payment if they will remove the ding from your credit report. They will usually counter with say, 75 percent and it just goes back and forth until both parties agree.

Now, tell the creditor to give you that in writing and you will pay the debt as soon as you receive the letter in the mail. Once you receive the offer in writing, be sure you honor your end of the agreement or you might find it difficult in dealing with the creditor again, because they will feel as if you did not keep your word. Remember that the idea is to turn a bad credit report into one that is good. Stick to any deals you made! If you offer the deal in writing, you can use letter eleven in the letters section as a guide.

Once you have the agreement in writing, and you make your payment, you now have something in writing from the creditor, or collector, as the case may be and if they do not honor their agreement, you can provide the letter to the credit bureau as proof of the deal.

Generally speaking, when it comes to tax liens, the only way to have those removed is to pay them off. Sometimes, as with the IRS, you can negotiate a lower amount to be paid. It does not hurt to ask, and if you give them the straight story on how it came to be that you got into this situation, they may actually lower the amount. It happens every day! In any case, you can likely have the lien removed before the debt is satisfied if you begin making agreed upon payments and you stick to a payment schedule.

By now, you have been taught how to remove most things from your report, thereby getting a better credit history. There are some things that you may have to simply have to wait out their allotted time before they will come off. These items include judgments, bankruptcies and other things like this. Persistence is the keep, and the credit bureau may simply remove such things without going to the trouble of verifying them. If they refuse to remove it from your record however, it will stay there for seven years, but must be removed after that. Generally speaking, all adverse information must be removed after seven years as far as that goes. Still, if you can have negative items removed sooner, then so-be-it. Also, there is no sense allowing anything to remain on your credit report longer than necessary, and the credit bureaus may not remove it until you request that they do so.

Letters in this Guide

Request for Credit Report
Request for Free Credit Report (based on credit denial)
Complaint Letter to Delete Inaccurate Information
Request for Removal of Outdated Information
Reminder to Respond
Request to Merge Credit Inquiries with Account
Demand for Corrected Credit Report
Addition of Consumer Statement
Request for Husband and Wife File Separation
Request for Addition of Supplementary Credit References
Explanation for Delinquent Payment
Creditor Settlement Agreement
Request for Reasons for Credit Denial

Sample Letter 1

RE: Request for Credit Report

To Whom it May Concern:

Please send me an up-to-date copy of my credit report. My details are as follows:

My Full Name is:

My Social Security Number is:

My Date of Birth is:

My Current Address is:

My Previous Address Was:

Enclosed, please find my check in the amount of $_____, as payment for the requested credit report. I have enclosed a copy of my identification as further verification of my identity.

Sincerely,

Sample Letter 2

RE: Request for Free Credit Report (based on denial of credit)

To Whom it May Concern:

Please send me a copy of my credit report as soon as possible. I have been denied credit based on information presented to a potential creditor through your company in the past 60-days. I have enclosed a copy of the denial letter that I received with this inquiry.

The Fair Credit Reporting Act of 1970, 15 USC section 1681g provides that the credit bureau should send me information which led to the rejection of my request for credit. According to the provisions of 15 USC section 1681j, there should be no charge for this report.

Sincerely,

Sample Letter 3

RE Complaint Letter to Delete Inaccurate Information

To Whom it May Concern:

I formally request that the following inaccurate items be immediately investigated. They must be removed in order to show my true credit history, as these items should not appear on my report. By the provisions of 15 USC section 1681i of the Fair Credit Reporting Act of 1970, I demand that these items be re-verified and deleted from my credit record:

Item No	Company Name	Account Number	Comments

Since 30 days from the time you receive this letter is the allotted time under the law to re-verify these entries, it should be understood that failure to do so within the 30-day period constitutes reason to promptly delete the information from my file (FCRA 15 USC s 1681i (5)(A)).

Also, pursuant to 15 USC s1681i (6)(A) of the Fair Credit Reporting Act, please notify me when the items have been deleted. You may send an updated copy of my credit report to the below address. According to 15 USC section 1681j, there should be no charge for this notification. Also, please send me names and addresses of individuals you have contacted so that I may follow-up with them.

Sincerely,

Sample Letter 4

RE: Request for Removal of Outdated Information

To Whom it May Concern:

Please note that under sections 605 and 607 of the Federal Fair Credit Reporting Act of 1970, you are obligated within 30 days to delete obsolete information from my consumer credit report. The following information appears on my credit report and the information is greater than seven years old.

Also, pursuant to section 168 of the same act, I am entitled to notification that the items have been removed and an updated copy of my credit report sent to me. The updated report can be sent to me at the address below and to any party who legitimately inquired about my credit history in the last 6 months.

I anticipate your full and immediate attention to this matter.

Sincerely,

Sample Letter 5

RE: Reminder to Respond

To Whom it May Concern:

Thirty days ago, you received a letter from me disputing several items on my credit report. The items were inaccurate and incomplete. Please find attached a copy of the original letter that I sent to your bureau.

Under the Federal Fair Credit Reporting Act of 1970, 15 USC 1681i (5)(A), you had 30 days from receipt of this letter to respond to my request for re-verification of the erroneous items. I have not yet received a reply from your bureau within these 30 days. Therefore, it must be that the information on my report was either inaccurate, or could not be verified. In any case, according to the provisions of 15 USC section 1681i (a), the items must be deleted immediately.

Please respond to this query immediately so that I do not feel compelled to pursue my legal rights under 15 USC section 1681n or 1681o, which require your compliance with the law.

Also, pursuant to 15 USC section 1681i (d) of the Fair Credit Reporting Act, please send me notification that the items have been deleted. Send an updated copy of my credit report to me at the address below, showing that the information has been updated as well as a copy to each of any other party who has legitimately requested my credit report in the last six months. According to USC section 1681j, there should be no charge for notification of any changes on my credit report.

Sincerely,

Sample Letter 6

RE: Request to Merge Inquiries with Accounts

To Whom it May Concern:

The presence of inquiries as entries separate from accounts on my credit report inaccurately duplicates information. These inquiries reflect an inaccurate processing of information in my file. The inquiry entries should be removed, or at least merged into the accounts to which they belong. The accounts in question are:

Company Name	Account Number

Under the provisions of the Federal Fair Credit Reporting Act of 1970, 15 USC section 1681i, please reinvestigate and delete these disputed items. Send me names and addresses of person contacted so that I may follow-up. Thirty days from receipt of this letter is the length of time permitted under 15 USC s1681i (5)(A) to complete these actions unless you immediately notify me otherwise. It should be understood that failure to reverify within this time frame constitutes non-verification under the law and the items must be promptly deleted.

Also, pursuant to 15 USC section 1681i(d) of the Fair Credit Reporting Act, please notify me when the items have been deleted and forward an updated copy of my credit report to me at the address below. According to 15 USC 1681j, there should be no charge for this updated information.

Sincerely,

Sample Letter 7

RE: Demand for Corrected Credit Report

To Whom it May Concern:

On _____, 20__, I wrote to tell you I had not heard about any specific action taken to reverify the items I had identified as inaccurate or incomplete in my credit report. Copies of my correspondence are attached for your review.

Since you have not provided me with names and addresses of the persons that you contacted for reverification of the information, nor have you complied within the statutory time period – 30 days – to my request for reverification, I assume that you have not been able to reverify the information that I have disputed. Therefore, you must comply with the provision of the Fair Credit Reporting Act and drop the disputed information from my credit report.

I demand that you send to me, and updated copy of my credit report showing that the information has been elimintated. According to 15 USC 1681j, there should be no charge for this updated credit report. The report must be postmarked no later than 5 days of your receipt of this letter, verified by your representative signing for it and the receipt returned to me.

If the updated report is not received by me within the allotted time, I will provide all necessary information to my attorney, who will follow-up in my place, at which time you will become liable for attorney fees and any other damages allowed to me by law under 15 USC section 1681n or 1681o of the Federal Fair Credit Reporting Act "Civial liability for willful noncompliance". Your bureau may then be liable for:

1) any actual damages I sustain from your failure to delete the items.
2) punitive damages as the court may allow
3) costs of court action, in addition to attorney's fees.

I have forwarded a copy of this letter to the Federal Trade Commission, the Subcommittee on Banking, Credit and Insurance, The _____ (enter your state) Consumer Protection Agency and Department of Business and Professional Regulations (Division of Consumer Complaints).

Sincerely,

Sample Letter 8

RE: Addition of Consumer Statement

To Whom it May Concern:

I have disputed the accuracy and completeness of incorrect information on my credit report. Since investigation has not resolved my dispute, I want the following statement, without alterations, included in my credit report to set forth the nature of my dispute for others to see:

According to the Federal Fair Credit Reporting Act of 1970, 15 USC section 1681i (b), I have the right to enter this "consumer statement" in my credit report. The Act also states that you are obligated to include my statement in any subsequent credit report that includes the disputed information. Furthermore, because my statement contains less than 100 words, I demand that yuou include the full text of the statement in my report, without changes, alterations or summaries.

Pursuant to the Fair Credit Reporting Act, please forward to me, free of charge, an updated credit report showing the information. I assume that 15 days from your receipt of this letter represents a reasonable period of time for completing this update, unless you notify me in writing immediately otherwise.

Sincerely,

Sample Letter 9

RE: Request for Husband and Wife Credit File Separation

To Whom it May Concern:

Current Account Number:

Under the Equal Opportunity Act, a husband and wife are allowed to maintain separate files pertaining to credit information. The undersigned request that credit information on the accounts of the undersigned be maintained in separate files.

We further request that all past, current and future information be reported as separate account information to all credit reporting agencies.

Sincerely,

_____   _____

_____   _____

Sample Letter 10

RE: request for Addition of Supplementary Credit References

To Whom it May Concern:

Pursuant to the Federal Fair Credit Reporting Act, 15 USC section 1681i, I am requesting that you add the following credit references to my credit report:

Creditors Name	Creditors Address	Account Number	Type of Account

Thank you in advance for your attention to this matter. Please inform me within the statutory 30-day time period from your receipt of this letter of your compliance with the 15 USC 1681e requirements that all information in a consumer's credit report be reflected with "… maximum possible accuracy."

Sincerely,

Sample Letter 11

RE: Explanation for Delinquent Payment

To Whom it May Concern

It has come to my attention that several of my payments to your account have been labeled "late" on my credit report.

These late payments were due to:

I have been prompt in paying in the past, and since the late payments occurred for the above excusable reason, I request that you please correct my payment history with the credit bureaus as shown here, which carry your account histories:

It is important that my credit report reflect the good relations I have had with your company in the past, and recently, and not the derogatory information present for just a couple of the payments. The corrections to my credit report will more accurately represent my normal financial habits.

I appreciate your assistance.

Sincerely,

Sample Letter 12

RE: Creditor Settlement Agreement

To Whom it May Concern:

I am writing to confirm our agreement regarding the settlement of a debt that I previously owed to your company. The terms that we agreed upon were:

1) I, _____, agree to pay _____ ("You"), the amount of $ _____ in full satisfaction of amounts that I owe to You, and You agree to accept this amount in full satisfaction of all amounts that I previously owed You.

2) I agree to pay the above amount in _____ monthly installments of $ _____ Without interest. The first payment to begin on _____ and each remaining payment on the _____ day of each following month. I will mail these payments to your office located at:

3) If I do not pay the full amount of each payment when it is due, I will be in default of our agreement. If I am in default, you may send me a written notice telling me that if I do not pay the overdue amount by a certain date, the entire unpaid balance will be due within 30 days after the date on which the notice is delivered or mailed to me.

4) Upon discharging this debt, you agree to notify each credit bureau to which you report credit information that any adverse credit information regarding my account with You is no longer verifiable and should be deleted from my credit report.

If you agree to the foregoing terms and conditions, please sign the Agreement and the enclosed copy in the places provided, and return the documents to me at the address below.

Accepted and Agreed
BY:_____
Name:_____
Title:_____

Sincerely,

Sample Letter 13

RE: Request for Reasons for Credit Denial

To Whom it May Concern:

Recently, the undersigned was denied credit by your company.

Please be advised that, pursuant to section 615(b) of the Federal Fair Credit Reporting Act of 1970, the undersigned hereby requests a full disclosure of the factual information disclosed to you by persons other than Consumer Reporting Agencies concerning the undersigned. Such information must be in sufficient detail to allow the undersigned to refute, challenge or dispute its accuracy.

Please take further notice that you are required to render such notification to the undersigned within a reasonable time. The Federal Trade Commission has defined such reasonable time as thirty (30) days.

Sincerely,

The Fair Credit Reporting Act

Sec. 1681. Congressional findings and statement of purpose

(a) The Congress makes the following findings:

    (1) The banking system is dependent upon fair and accurate credit reporting. Inaccurate credit reports directly impair the efficiency of the banking system, and unfair credit reporting methods undermine the public confidence which is essential to the continued functioning of the banking system.

    (2) An elaborate mechanism has been developed for investigating and evaluating the credit worthiness, credit standing, credit capacity, character, and general reputation of consumers.

    (3) Consumer reporting agencies have assumed a vital role in assembling and evaluating consumer credit and other information on consumers.

    (4) There is a need to insure that consumer reporting agencies exercise their grave responsibilities with fairness, impartiality, and a respect for the consumer's right to privacy.

(b) It is the purpose of this title to require that consumer reporting agencies adopt reasonable procedures for meeting the needs of commerce for consumer credit, personnel, insurance, and other information in a manner which is fair and equitable to the consumer, with regard to the confidentiality, accuracy, relevancy, and proper utilization of such information in accordance with the requirements of this title.

Sec. 1681a. Definitions; rules of construction

(a) Definitions and rules of construction set forth in this section are applicable for the purposes of this title.

(b) The term "person" means any individual, partnership, corporation, trust, estate, cooperative, association, government or governmental subdivision or agency, or other entity.

(c) The term "consumer" means an individual.

(d) The term "consumer report" means any written, oral, or other communication of any information by a consumer reporting agency bearing on a consumer's credit worthiness, credit standing, credit capacity, character, general reputation, personal characteristics, or mode of living which is used or expected to be used or collected in whole or in part for the purpose of serving as a factor in establishing the consumer's eligibility for (1) credit or insurance to be used primarily for personal, family, or household purposes, or (2) employment purposes, or (3) other purposes authorized under section 604. The term does not include (A) any report containing information solely as to transactions or experiences between the consumer and the person making the report; (B) any authorization or approval of a specific extension of credit directly or indirectly by the issuer of a credit card or similar device; or (C) any report in which a person who has been requested by a third party to make a specific extension of credit directly or indirectly to a

consumer conveys his decision with respect to such request, if the third party advises the consumer of the name and address of the person to whom the request was made and such person makes the disclosures to the consumer required under section 615

(e) The term "investigative consumer report" means a consumer report or portion thereof in which information on a consumer's character, general reputation, personal characteristics, or mode of living is obtained through personal interviews with neighbors, friends, or associates of the consumer reported on or with others with whom he is acquainted or who may have knowledge concerning any such items of information. However, such information shall not include specific factual information on a consumer's credit record obtained directly from a creditor of the consumer or from a consumer reporting agency when such information was obtained directly from a creditor of the consumer or from the consumer.

(f) The term "consumer reporting agency" means any person which, for monetary fees, dues, or on a cooperative nonprofit basis, regularly engages in whole or in part in the practice of assembling or evaluating consumer credit information or other information on consumers for the purpose of furnishing consumer reports to third parties, and which uses any means or facility of interstate commerce for the purpose of preparing or furnishing consumer reports.

(g) The term "file," when used in connection with information on any consumer, means all of the information on that consumer recorded and retained by a consumer reporting agency regardless of how the information is stored.

(h) The term "employment purposes" when used in connection with a consumer report means a report used for the purpose of evaluating a consumer for employment, promotion, reassignment or retention as an employee.

(i) The term "medical information" means information or records obtained, with the consent of the individual to whom it relates, from licensed physicians or medical practitioners, hospitals, clinics, or other medical or medically related facilities.

Sec. 1681b. Permissible purposes of consumer reports

A consumer reporting agency may furnish a consumer report under the following circumstances and no other:

(1) In response to the order of a court having jurisdiction to issue such an order, or a subpoena issued in connection with proceedings before a Federal grand jury.

(2) In accordance with the written instructions of the consumer to whom it relates.

(3) To a person which it has reason to believe--

> (A) intends to use the information in connection with a credit transaction involving the consumer on whom the information is to be furnished and involving the extension of credit to, or review or collection of an account of, the consumer; or
>
> (B) intends to use the information for employment purposes; or
>
> (C) intends to use the information in connection with the underwriting of insurance involving the consumer; or
>
> (D) intends to use the information in connection with a determination of the consumer's eligibility for a license or other benefit granted by a governmental instrumentality required by law to consider an applicant's financial responsibility or status; or
>
> (E) otherwise has a legitimate business need for the information in connection with a business transaction involving the consumer.

Sec. 1681c. Reporting of obsolete information prohibited

(a) Except as authorized under subsection (b), no consumer reporting agency may make any consumer report containing any of the following items of information:

> (1) cases under title 11 of the United States Code or under the Bankruptcy Act that, from the date of entry of the order for relief or the date of adjudication, as the case may be, antedate the report by more than 10 years.
>
> (2) Suits and judgments which, from date of entry, antedate the report by more than seven years or until the governing statute of limitations has expired, whichever is the longer period.
>
> (3) Paid tax liens which, from date of payment, antedate the report by more than seven years.
>
> (4) Accounts placed for collection or charged to profit and loss which antedate the report by more than seven years.
>
> (5) Records of arrest, indictment, or conviction of crime which, from date of disposition, release, or parole, antedate the report by more than seven years.
>
> (6) Any other adverse item of information which antedates the report by more than seven years.

(b) The provisions of subsection (a) are not applicable in the case of any consumer credit report to be used in connection with--

(1) a credit transaction involving, or which may reasonably be expected to involve, a principal amount of $ 50,000 or more;

(2) the underwriting of life insurance involving, or which may reasonably be expected to involve, a face amount of $ 50,000 or more; or

(3) the employment of any individual at an annual salary which equals, or which may reasonably be expected to equal $ 20,000, or more.

Sec. 1681d. Disclosure of investigative consumer reports

(a) Disclosure of fact of preparation. A person may not procure or cause to be prepared an investigative consumer report on any consumer unless--

(1) it is clearly and accurately disclosed to the consumer that an investigative consumer report including information as to his character, general reputation, personal characteristics and mode of living, whichever are applicable, may be made, and such disclosure (A) is made in a writing mailed, or otherwise delivered, to the consumer, not later than three days after the date on which the report was first requested, and (B) includes a statement informing the consumer of his right to request the additional disclosures provided for under subsection (b) of this section; or

(2) the report is to be used for employment purposes for which the consumer has not specifically applied.

(b) Disclosure on request of nature and scope of investigation. Any person who procures or causes to be prepared an investigative consumer report on any consumer shall, upon written request made by the consumer within a reasonable period of time after the receipt by him of the disclosure required by subsection (a) (1), shall make a complete and accurate disclosure of the nature and scope of the investigation requested. This disclosure shall be made in a writing mailed, or otherwise delivered, to the consumer not later than five days after the date on which the request for such disclosure was received from the consumer or such report was first requested, whichever is the later.

(c) Limitation on liability upon showing of reasonable procedures for compliance with provisions. No person may be held liable for any violation of subsection (a) or (b) of this section if he shows by a preponderance of the evidence that at the time of the violation he maintained reasonable procedures to assure compliance with subsection (a) or (b).

Sec. 1681e. Compliance procedures

(a) Every consumer reporting agency shall maintain reasonable procedures designed to avoid violations of section 605 and to limit the furnishing of consumer reports to the purposes listed under section 604 . These procedures shall require that prospective users of the information identify themselves, certify the purposes for which the information is sought, and certify that the information will be used for no other purpose.

Every consumer reporting agency shall make a reasonable effort to verify the identity of a new prospective user and the uses certified by such prospective user prior to furnishing such user a consumer report. No consumer reporting agency may furnish a consumer report to any person if it has reasonable grounds for believing that the consumer report will not be used for a purpose listed in section 604 .

(b) Whenever a consumer reporting agency prepares a consumer report it shall follow reasonable procedures to assure maximum possible accuracy of the information concerning the individual about whom the report relates.

Sec. 1681f. Disclosures to governmental agencies

Notwithstanding the provisions of section 604, a consumer reporting agency may furnish identifying information respecting any consumer, limited to his name, address, former addresses, places of employment, or former places of employment, to a governmental agency.

S. 1681g. Disclosures to consumers

(a) Every consumer reporting agency shall, upon request and proper identification of any consumer, clearly and accurately disclose to the consumer:

> (1) The nature and substance of all information (except medical information) in its files on the consumer at the time of the request.

> (2) The sources of the information; except that the sources of information acquired solely for use in preparing an investigative consumer report and actually used for no other purpose need not be disclosed: Provided, That in the event an action is brought under this title, such sources shall be available to the plaintiff under appropriate discovery procedures in the court in which the action is brought.

> (3) The recipients of any consumer report on the consumer which it has furnished--
>> (A) for employment purposes within the two-year period preceding the request, and
>> (B) for any other purpose within the six-month period preceding the request.

(b) The requirements of subsection (a) respecting the disclosure of sources of information and the recipients of consumer reports do not apply to information received or consumer reports furnished prior to the effective date of this title except to the extent that the matter involved is contained in the files of the consumer reporting agency on that date.

Sec. 1681h. Conditions of disclosure to consumers

(a) Times and notice. A consumer reporting agency shall make the disclosures required under section 609 during normal business hours and on reasonable notice.

(b) Identification of consumer. The disclosures required under section 609 shall be made to the consumer--

(1) in person if he appears in person and furnishes proper identification; or

(2) by telephone if he has made a written request, with proper identification, for telephone disclosure and the toll charge, if any, for the telephone call is prepaid by or charged directly to the consumer.

(c) Trained personnel. Any consumer reporting agency shall provide trained personnel to explain to the consumer any information furnished to him pursuant to section 609.

(d) Persons accompanying consumer. The consumer shall be permitted to be accompanied by one other person of his choosing, who shall furnish reasonable identification. A consumer reporting agency may require the consumer to furnish a written statement granting permission to the consumer reporting agency to discuss the consumer's file in such person's presence.

(e) Limitation of liability. Except as provided in sections 616 and 617 , no consumer may bring any action or proceeding in thenature of defamation, invasion of privacy, or negligence with respect to the reporting of information against any consumer reporting agency, any user of information, or any person who furnishes information to a consumer reporting agency, based on information disclosed pursuant to section 609, 610, or 615, except as to false information furnished with malice or willful intent to injure such consumer.

Sec. 1681i. Procedure in case of disputed accuracy

(a) Dispute; reinvestigation. If the completeness or accuracy of any item of information contained in his file is disputed by a consumer, and such dispute is directly conveyed to the consumer reporting agency by the consumer, the consumer reporting agency shall within a reasonable period of time reinvestigate and record the current status of that information unless it has reasonable grounds to believe that the dispute by the consumer is frivolous or irrelevant. If after such reinvestigation such information is found to be inaccurate or can no longer be verified, the consumer reporting agency shall promptly delete such information. The presence of contradictory information in the consumer's file does not in and of itself constitute reasonable grounds for believing the dispute is frivolous or irrelevant.

(b) Statement of dispute. If the reinvestigation does not resolve the dispute, the consumer may file a brief statement setting forth the nature of the dispute. The consumer reporting agency may limit such statements to not more than one hundred words if it provides the consumer with assistance in writing a clear summary of the dispute.

(c) Notification of consumer dispute in subsequent consumer reports. Whenever a statement of a dispute is filed, unless there is reasonable grounds to believe that it is frivolous or irrelevant, the consumer reporting agency shall, in any subsequent consumer report containing the information in question, clearly note that it is disputed by the consumer and provide either the consumer's statement or a clear and accurate codification or summary thereof.

(d) Notification of deletion of disputed information. Following any deletion of information which is found to be inaccurate or whose accuracy can no longer be verified or any notation as to disputed information, the consumer reporting agency shall, at the request of the consumer, furnish notification that the port for any item has been deleted or the statement, codification or summary pursuant to subsection (b) or (c) to any person specifically designated by the consumer who has within two years prior thereto received a consumer report for employment purposes, or within six months prior thereto received a consumer re other purpose, which contained the deleted or disputed information. The consumer reporting agency shall clearly and conspicuously disclose to the consumer his rights to make such a request. Such disclosure shall be made at or prior to the time the information is deleted or the consumer's statement regarding the disputed information is received.

Sec. 1681j. Charges for disclosures

A consumer reporting agency shall make all disclosures pursuant to section 609 and furnish all consumer reports pursuant to section 611(d) without charge to the consumer if, within thirty days after receipt by such consumer of a notification pursuant to section 615 or notification from a debt collection agency affiliated with such consumer reporting agency stating that the consumer's credit rating may be or has been adversely affected, the consumer makes a request under section 609 or 611(d) . Otherwise, the consumer reporting agency may impose a reasonable charge on the consumer for making disclosure to such consumer pursuant to section 609 , the charge for which shall be indicated to the consumer prior to making disclosure; and for furnishing notifications, statements, summaries, or codifications to person designated by the consumer pursuant to section 611(d), the charge for which shall be indicated to the consumer prior to furnishing such information and shall not exceed the charge that the consumer reporting agency would impose on each designated recipient for a consumer report except that no charge may be made for notifying such persons of the deletion of information which is found to be inaccurate or which can no longer be verified.

Sec. 1681k. Public record information for employment purposes

A consumer reporting agency which furnishes a consumer report for employment purposes and which for that purpose compiles and reports items of information on consumers which are matters of public record and are likely to have an adverse effect upon a consumer's ability to obtain employment shall--

(1) at the time such public record information is reported to the user of such consumer report, notify the consumer of the fact that public record information is being reported by the consumer reporting agency, together with the name and address of the person to whom such information is being reported; or

(2) maintain strict procedures designed to insure that whenever public record information which is likely to have an adverse effect on a consumer's ability to obtain employment is reported it is complete and up to date. For purposes of this paragraph, items of public record relating to arrests, indictments, convictions, suits, tax liens, and outstanding judgments shall be considered up to date if the current public record status of the item at the time of the report is reported.

Sec. 1681l. Restrictions on investigative consumer reports

Whenever a consumer reporting agency prepares an investigative consumer report, no adverse information in the consumer report (other than information which is a matter of public record) may be included in a subsequent consumer report unless such adverse information has been verified in the process of making such subsequent consumer report, or the adverse information was received within the three-month period preceding the date the subsequent report is furnished.

Sec. 1681m. Requirements on users of consumer reports

(a) Adverse action based on reports of consumer reporting agencies. Whenever credit or insurance for personal, family, or household purposes, or employment involving a consumer is denied or the charge for such credit or insurance is increased either wholly or partly because of information contained in a consumer report from a consumer reporting agency, the user of the consumer report shall so advise the consumer against whom such adverse action has been taken and supply the name and address of the consumer reporting agency making the report.

(b) Adverse action based on reports of persons other than consumer reporting agencies. Whenever credit for personal, family, or household purposes involving a consumer is denied or the charge for such credit is increased either wholly or partly because of information obtained from a person other than a consumer reporting agency bearing upon the consumer's credit worthiness, credit standing, credit capacity, character, general reputation, personal characteristics, or mode of living, the user of such information shall, within a reasonable period of time, upon the consumer's written request for the reasons for such adverse action received within sixty days after learning of such adverse action, disclose the nature of the information to the consumer. The user of such information shall clearly and accurately disclose to the consumer his right to make such written request at the time such adverse action is communicated to the consumer.

(c) Reasonable procedures to assure compliance. No person shall be held liable for any violation of this section if he shows by a preponderance of the evidence that at the time of the alleged violation he maintained reasonable procedures to assure compliance with the provisions of subsections (a) and (b).

Sec. 1681n. Civil liability for willful noncompliance

Any consumer reporting agency or user of information which willfully fails to comply with any requirement imposed under this title with respect to any consumer is liable to that consumer in an amount equal to the sum of--

(1) any actual damages sustained by the consumer as a result of the failure;

(2) such amount of punitive damages as the court may allow; and

(3) in the case of any successful action to enforce any liability under this section, the costs of the action together with reasonable attorney's fees as determined by the court.

Sec. 1681o. Civil liability for negligent noncompliance

Any consumer reporting agency or user of information which is negligent in failing to comply with any requirement imposed under this title with respect to any consumer is liable to that consumer in an amount equal to the sum of--

(1) any actual damages sustained by the consumer as a result of the failure;

(2) in the case of any successful action to enforce any liability under this section, the costs of the action together with reasonable attorney's fees as determined by the court.

Sec. 1681p. Jurisdiction of courts; limitation of actions

An action to enforce any liability created under this title may be brought in any appropriate United States district court without regard to the amount in controversy, or in any other court of competent jurisdiction, within two years from the date on which the liability arises, except that where a defendant has materially and willfully misrepresented any information required under this title to be disclosed to an individual and the information so misrepresented is material to the establishment of the defendant's liability to that individual under this title, the action may be brought at any time within two years after discovery by the individual of the misrepresentation.

Sec. 1681q. Obtaining information under false pretenses

Any person who knowingly and willfully obtains information on a consumer from a consumer reporting agency under false pretenses shall be fined not more than $ 5,000 or imprisoned not more than one year, or both.

Sec. 1681r. Unauthorized disclosures by officers or employees

Any officer or employee of a consumer reporting agency who knowingly and willfully provides information concerning an individual from the agency's files to a person not authorized to receive that information shall be fined not more than $ 5,000 or imprisoned not more than one year, or both.
Sec. 1681s. Administrative enforcement
(a) Federal Trade Commission; powers. Compliance with the requirements imposed under this title shall be enforced under the Federal Trade Commission Act by the Federal Trade Commission with respect to consumer reporting agencies and all other persons subject thereto, except to the extent that enforcement of the requirements imposed under this title is specifically committed to some other government agency under subsection (b) hereof.
For the purpose of the exercise by the Federal Trade Commission of its functions and powers under the Federal Trade Commission Act, a violation of any requirement or prohibition imposed under this title shall constitute an unfair or deceptive act or practice in commerce in violation of section 5(a) of the Federal Trade Commission Act and shall be subject to enforcement by the Federal Trade Commission under section 5(b) thereof with respect to any consumer reporting agency or person

subject to enforcement by the Federal Trade Commission pursuant to this subsection, irrespective of whether that person is engaged in commerce or meets any other jurisdictional tests in the Federal Trade Commission Act. The Federal Trade Commission shall have such procedural, investigative, and enforcement powers, including the power to issue procedural rules in enforcing compliance with the requirements imposed under this title and to require the filing of reports, the production of documents, and the appearance of witnesses as though the applicable terms and conditions of the Federal Trade Commission Act were part of this title. Any person violating any of the provisions of this title shall be subject to the penalties and entitled to the privileges and immunities provided in the Federal Trade Commission Act as though the applicable terms and provisions thereof were part of this title.

(b) Other administrative bodies. Compliance with the requirements imposed under this title with respect to consumer reporting agencies and persons who use consumer reports from such agencies shall be enforced under--

> (1) section 8 of the Federal Deposit Insurance Act, in the case of--
>> (A) national banks, and Federal branches and Federal agencies of foreign banks, by the Office of the Comptroller of the Currency;
>>
>> (B) member banks of the Federal Reserve System (other than national banks), branches and agencies of foreign banks (other than Federal branches, Federal agencies, and insured State branches of foreign banks), commercial lending companies owned or controlled by foreign banks, and organizations operating under section 25 or 25(a)of the Federal Reserve Act , by the Board of Governors of the Federal Reserve System; and
>>
>> (C) banks insured by the Federal Deposit Insurance Corporation (other than members of the Federal Reserve System) and insured State branches of foreign banks, by the Board of Directors of the Federal Deposit Insurance Corporation.
>
> (2) section 8 of the Federal Deposit Insurance Act, by the Director of the Office of Thrift Supervision, in the case of a savings association the deposits of which are insured by the Federal Deposit Insurance Corporation;
>
> (3) the Federal Credit Union Act, by the Administrator of the National Credit Union Administration with respect to any Federal credit union;
>
> (4) the Acts to regulate commerce, by the Interstate Commerce Commission with respect to any common carrier subject to those Acts;
>
> (5) the Federal Aviation Act of 1958, by the Secretary of Transportation with respect to any air carrier or foreign air carrier subject to that Act ; and
>
> (6) the Packers and Stockyards Act, 1921(except as provided in section 406 of that Act), by the Secretary of Agriculture with respect to any activities subject to that Act.
>
> The terms used in paragraph (1) that are not defined in this title or otherwise defined in section 3(s) of the Federal Deposit Insurance Act (12 U.S.C. 1813(s)) shall have the meaning given to them in section 1(b) of the International Banking Act of 1978 (12 U.S.C. 3101).

(c) Enforcement under other authority. For the purpose of the exercise by any agency referred to in subsection (b) of its powers under any Act referred to in that subsection, a violation of any requirement imposed under this title shall be deemed to be a violation of a requirement imposed under that Act. In addition to its powers under any provision of law specifically referred to in subsection (b), each of the agencies referred to in that subsection may exercise, for the purpose of enforcing compliance with any requirement imposed under this title any other authority conferred on it by law.

Sec. 1681t. Relation to State laws

This title does not annul, alter, affect, or exempt any person subject to the provisions of this title from complying with the laws of any State with respect to the collection, distribution, or use of any information on consumers, except to the extent that those laws are inconsistent with any provision of this title, and then only to the extent of the inconsistency.

Banks that Will Open a Checking Account When you are in ChexSystems Or Telecheck

When you use this section, be aware that information in today's society changes rapidly. At the time this book went to press, the information was accurate, however, it is possible that some of it changed even before the book was printed. To this end, the publisher nor the author can guarantee that any of the information contained in the pages is still viable.

ALABAMA
Compass Bank (uses Telecheck)
Suntrust Bank (uses Telecheck)
Alabama Central Credit Union
Alabama Telco Credit Union
America's First Federal Credit Union
Ameris Bank
Armed Forces Bank
BB&T
Florence Federal Credit Union
Merchant's Bank
Renasant Bank
Whitney Bank

ALASKA
Alaska Pacific Bank
Matanuska Valley Federal Credit Union
Mount Mckinley Bank
Northrim Bank
Spirit of America Federal Credit Union
True North Federal Credit Union

ARIZONA
Desert Schools Federal Credit Union
Arizona Federal Credit Union
Armed Forces Bank

ARKANSAS
Arvest Bank
Bank of the Ozarks
Bank of America

CALIFORNIA
Technology Credit Union
Golden 1 Credit Union
San Francisco Federal Credit Union
San Mateo Credit Union
US Bank
Broadway Federal Bank
Bank of America
Matadors Community Credit Union
First Entertainment Credit Union
Wescom Credit Union
Schools First Federal Credit Union
California Credit Union
Orange County Federal Credit Union
California Bank and trust
Wells Fargo Bank

COLORADO
First United Bank
Bank of Denver
Equitable Savings & Loan Association
Credit Union of Denver
Elevations Credit Union
Partner Colorado Credit Union
Valley Bank and Trust
Armed Forces Bank

CONNECTICUT
Marlborough Savings Bank
Savings Institute
Navy Federal Credit Union

DELAWARE
Fort Sill National Bank

FLORIDA
Gold Coast Federal Credit Union
Compass Bank
Bank United
City National Bank of Florida
GTE Federal Credit Union
Florida State Employees Federal Credit Union
Members First Credit Union of Florida
Fifth Third Bank
1st National Bank of South Florida
Navy Federal Credit Union

GEORGIA
Ameris Bank
Armed Forces Bank
BB&T Bank
Columbus Bank and Trust
Excel Federal Credit Union
First Tennessee Bank
Navy Federal Credit Union
Suntrust Bank (Uses Telecheck)

HAWAII
Navy Federal Credit Union

IDAHO
Capital Educators Federal Credit Union
Cottonwood Community Credit Union
Global Credit Union
Horizon Credit Union
Idaho Central Credit Union
Latah Federal Credit Union
Mountain West Bank
Pine Tree Community Credit Union
Pioneer Federal Credit Union
Sterling Savings Bank

ILLINOIS
Armed Forces bank
Catlin Bank
Hawthorne Bank
Hebron State Bank
TCF National Bank
Navy Federal Credit Union

INDIANA
Century Bank & Trust
Fifth Third Bank
TCF Bank

IOWA
First State Bank of Colfax
First American Bank

KANSAS
Metcalf Bank
Armed Forces Bank

KENTUCKY
Armed Forces Bank
Fifth Third Bank
Park National Bank
River City Bank

LOUISIANNA
CSE Federal Credit Union
Whitney National Bank
Navy Federal Credit Union

MAINE
Bank of New Hampshire

MARYLAND
Navy Federal Credit Union
Suntrust Bank (uses Telecheck)
Wells Fargo Bank

MASSACUSETTS
Bank of New England
Charter One

MICHIGAN
Century Bank and Trust
Charter One Bank
Credit Union One
TCF Bank

MINNESOTA
TCF National Bank
Wells Fargo Bank

MISSISSIPPI
First Tennessee Bank
Regions Bank
Renasant Bank
Suntrust Bank (uses Telecheck)
Whitney Bank

MISSOURI
Armed Forces Bank
Arvest Bank
Bank of Kirksville
Electro Savings CU
Rockwood Bank
St John's Bank and Trust

MONTANA
1st United Bank
Adrian State Bank
Alerus Financial
Alliance Bank
Altra Federal Credit Union
BestBank
Big Sky Western Bank
BNC National Bank
Fallon County Federal Credit Union
First Minnentonka City Bank
First Security Bank
Garfield County Bank
Gateway Community Federal Credit Union
Marquette Bank
Topline Federal Credit Union

NEBRASKA
Farmer's State Bank
Fremont National Bank and Trust
Neighborhood Federal Credit Union
PNC Bank

NEVADA
Armed Forces National Bank
Branch Banking and Trust Company
First Entertainment Credit Union
Nevada State Bank

NEW HAMPSHIRE
Bank of New England
Bank of New Hampshire

NEW JERSEY
ABCO Public Employees Federal Credit Union
Armed Forces Bank
Navy Federal Credit Union

NEW MEXICO
Bank 34
Bank of Albuquerque
BOK Financial Corporation
Commerce Bank
Compass Bank
First National Bank of New Mexico
Jemez Valley Credit Union
New Mexico Educators Credit Union
U.S. New Mexico Federal Credit Union

NEW YORK
Abacus Federal Savings Bank
United Orient Bank
Allied Irish Bank
Alternatives Federal Credit Union
Bank of New Hampshire
Charter One
Community Bank
Cross Country Federal Savings Bank
Fulton Savings Bank
Great Eastern Bank
Horizons Federal Credit Union
Ticonderoga Federal Credit Union
Tompkins County Trust Company
Trustco Bank

NORTH CAROLINA
First Citizens Bank
State Employees Credit Union
Fort Sill National Bank
Self-Help Credit Union
Navy Federal Credit Union

NORTH DAKOTA
Armed Forces Bank
PNC Bank

OHIO
Century Bank and Trust
Charter One Bank
Cintel Federal Credit Union
Fifth Third Bank
First Day Federal Credit Union
Park National Bank
Navy Federal Credit Union

OKLAHOMA
First National Bank of Midwest City
City National Bank
Arvest Bank
Yukon National Bank
Fort Sill National Bank
Fort Sill Federal Credit Union

OREGON
Oregon Community Credit Union

PENNSYLVANIA
1st Summit Bank
Dollar Bank
Philadelphia Federal Credit Union
Navy Federal Credit Union
PNC Bank

RHODE ISLAND
Rhode Island Credit Union
Navy Federal Credit Union

SOUTH CAROLINA
Ameris Bank
First Federal Bank
Fort Sill National Bank
Mutual Savings Bank
Navy Federal Credit Union

SOUTH DAKOTA
Dakota State Bank
F&M State Bank
First Dakota National Bank
Dakota Plains Federal Credit Union
East River Federal Credit Union
Northern Hills Federal Credit Union
Sentinel Federal Credit Union

TENNESSEE
First Tennessee Bank
PNC Bank
Suntrust Bank (uses Telecheck)
Navy Federal Credit Union

TEXAS
Bank of Houston (uses Telecheck)
First Convenience Banks
Austin Telco Federal Credit Union
Chase Bank of Texas
Bank United
Compass Bank
Credit Union of Texas
Texas Bank
Metro Bank
Frost Bank
Armed Forces Bank
Fort Sill National Bank

Texas (continued)
Navy Federal Credit Union

UTAH
Family First Federal Credit Union
Alliance Credit union
Alpine Credit Union
Cyprus Credit Union
Grantsville Federal Credit Union
Jordan Credit Union
MetroWest Credit Union
Transwest Credit Union
PNC Bank

VERMONT
Charter One
Bank of New Hampshire

VIRGINIA
Suntrust Bank (uses Telecheck)
First Citizen's Bank
First Tennessee Bank
Navy Federal Credit Union

WASHINGTON
Sterling Savings Bank
Harborstone Credit Union
Qualstar Credit Union
First Mutual Bank
Armed Forces Bank
Navy Federal Credit Union

WEST VIRGINIA
First Citizen Bank
Susquehanna Bank

WISCONSIN
Wells Fargos Bank
TCF National Bank
Westbury Savings Bank
Denmark State Bank
First Community Bank
FirstMerit Bank
Nicolet National Bank
River Valley Bank
Bank of Mauston
Best Bank
Community Bank and Trust
DMB Community Bank
Farmers Savings Bank
RiverWood-Maritime Credit Union
Altra Federal Credit Union
WestConsin Credit Union
CoVantage Credit Union
Dane County Credit Union
Fox Communities Credit Union
Marine Credit Union
Prospera Credit Union
RIA Federal Credit Union

WYOMING
1st Bank
ACPE Federal Credit Union
Armed Forces Bank
Bank of Commerce
Bank of Jackson Hole
Meridian Trust Federal Credit Union
Sundance State Bank
United People's Federal Credit Union
Western Vista Federal Credit Union

Many banks will also offer second chance checking accounts regardless of whether you appear on a ChexSystems or Telecheck report or not. Look around at local banks and try to open accounts in person so that you are able to explain away any hits the bank might get when opening your account.

About the Author

Stephen Steinberger holds a MS in Finance from Kaplan University and spends his time helping people to recover from financial disasters such as the great recession the US experienced beginning in 2007.

He has helped countless people repair their credit history and assisted many in buying a new home once the reports are straightened out. This is his first book, written with the struggling consumer in mind, to help them get back on their feet financially.

www.ingramcontent.com/pod-product-compliance
Lightning Source LLC
Chambersburg PA
CBHW080941040426
42444CB00015B/3395